2023

MW00932415

Angel -
Hustle
Dream BIG -
Do BIG !
Matt

THE OTHER SIDE

From a Shack to Silicon Valley

By: Martha Niño Rodriguez

ISBN: 9798362830410

Author: Martha Niño Rodriguez
Artist for Book Cover: Aniko Balogh
Edited and Designed by Rising Above Publishing Services

QUANTITY PURCHASES: Schools, companies, professional groups, clubs,
and other organizations may qualify for special terms when ordering bulk quantities of this title. Contact the author at: www.marthanino.com

Shack

[shack] NOUN

a roughly built hut or cabin.

I was born in a shack in a small village named Pueblo Viejo (Old Town) in Mexico, and old it really was. It was also very poor. How poor? The shack was held together with mud and grass and the floors were dirt. There was no drinking water or electricity. I never had a real crib. My crib was an old dresser drawer. Being poor in a third-world country is so different than being poor in the United States.

Education is also different in Mexico. Depending on a child's situation, you may go to school very little, if at all, and be forced to work at a very young age. My father got as far as the second grade and my mother went up to the sixth. The poor are left to live uneducated and all that's left to do is work or start a family – no matter your age.

My parents were married young. Mom was only 16 and my dad a few years older. To survive, they picked cotton. Working in the fields in the U.S. is tough, but working in the fields in Mexico, well, it's brutal to say the least. This is the type of work my parents did. As you can imagine, surviving with minimal money or knowledge was definitely a challenge. I was not even two years old when my parents decided there was no future for me in Mexico. They were about to make the hardest decision of their lives.

No, this was not a legal, documented plane adventure they were about to take. Consider yourself fortunate if you can travel like this. With the little money they had, and money borrowed from family they hired "Coyotes" (people smugglers) to guide us to the other side – The United States. The plan was for my parents to walk along the country's borders, hide and be silent until it was safe to cross. Meanwhile, I would be passing as a stranger's "Coyote's" daughter in a car. Both plans needed to align – the hope was to reunite. HOPE. Like many of you reading this – you probably had a family member that started life in a different place. This start broke the cycle of where you would have been to where you are now. Let's be grateful. They might have come here on planes, some by boats, some on a train, some by car or like my parents by foot. They were the first. Being the first and knowing very little about a foreign country comes with its challenges, it's also scary and very risky. I know the United States is not perfect, but for many it's better and better is worth the risk. For me, the risk paid off and my life is better, but for many, better never happens because HOPE is cut short.

The other day, I was reading the news and at the bottom of the page there was an article. The title of the article was, "Migrants Found Dead in Abandoned Truck in Texas," - over 50 humans lost their lives packed in a truck. No one ever came to their rescue. There were 39 men, 12 women, and the temperature outside was 103 degrees. I'm sure they yelled and yelled, and no one heard their screams. Trapped in a metal box, there was no air ... hot temperatures ... they died hoping.

Imagine.

Let's reflect on how fortunate we are, that we have water, electricity ... air. It's something many risk their lives to have. There are far too many stories like this but sadly they are hidden, put at the bottom of the paper, and silenced.

My youngest asked me about the case in Texas, with tears in my eyes, all I could tell her was … "They are why I speak and write. I am them. She is them. There are humans but despite their yells, they cannot be heard. They need someone else to scream for them." She nodded and understood.

Speaking and writing about coming from dirt in its rawest form is important. We are humans that can add value - all we need is for others to see the value in us. We need them to open the door. One door can make a difference. One.

DEDICATION

I have been very fortunate. My parents took a risk that paid off. They wanted a better life for me – and I have it. I have managed to get from that shack in Mexico to representing top Silicon Valley technology companies in the world and I did this even though: I was undocumented; I lived in poverty; I was born from parents with minimal education; I lived in a one-bedroom home with eight other people; I didn't know English; I failed all my classes; I was considered a "bad influence"; I got kicked out of high school; my father died; I was once silent, but there are other facts, too.

There are facts like: Good people sat me down and showed me a path; good people asked me WHY so they could better help me; good people looked beyond the surface and saw something in me; good people gave me an opportunity; I entered tech not knowing tech; I am part of the only ~2% of Latinas in the Tech Industry; I learned new skills by being curious; I broke the cycle of poverty; I broke the cycle of silence; good people and kind words made me feel "safe" with all my life facts.

What are your facts? Let's look at all of them and own them because they happened. Let's take the taboo away from HURT and turn it into HOPE. To all the good people (my believers and even my non-believers) that my life path has crossed, you are no accident. I am grateful for all of you. You were put in my life for a reason. This book is for you.

To my parents who took the biggest risk of all, which was our lives, from the bottom of my heart, I thank you. My life is better because of you and the lives of the generations that follow me will be better too. You started a good thing ... this book is for you.

To the children reading this, may this book be proof that where you may be or where you have been does not define how far you can get. This book is for you. To those who feel less than - this book is for you. To those who see beauty in the broken – this book is for you. To the millions of immigrants in search of a better life, the ones that have made it, the ones that will make it, and the good humans that will help us get there – this book is for you. To the immigrants that leave everything for a better life relying on HOPE and never make it, because hope is not enough, sometimes we need others – this book is for you.

To my family and friends, thank you for being with me through thick and thin on this life journey – this book is for you. To my daughters Kiana and Keila, you are why I do everything. Believe in yourselves, even when someone else does not believe in you. If it feels right, then do it and don't stop for anything. Let that good feeling be your guiding light to everything. I love you so much – this book is for you. ~ Love mom.

Enjoy this collection of short stories and reflections from my life. The memories I didn't want to forget; all have been written from the heart. They all are real and all are raw. These are stories and reflections of hope, of hurt, some funny, some sad, but all in effort to show value in coming from "different". A perspective from the once silenced, a perspective from someone who comes from somewhere else, a perspective from "THE OTHER SIDE."

Peace, love and humanity everyone.

Me in the early 70's upon arrival to the United States

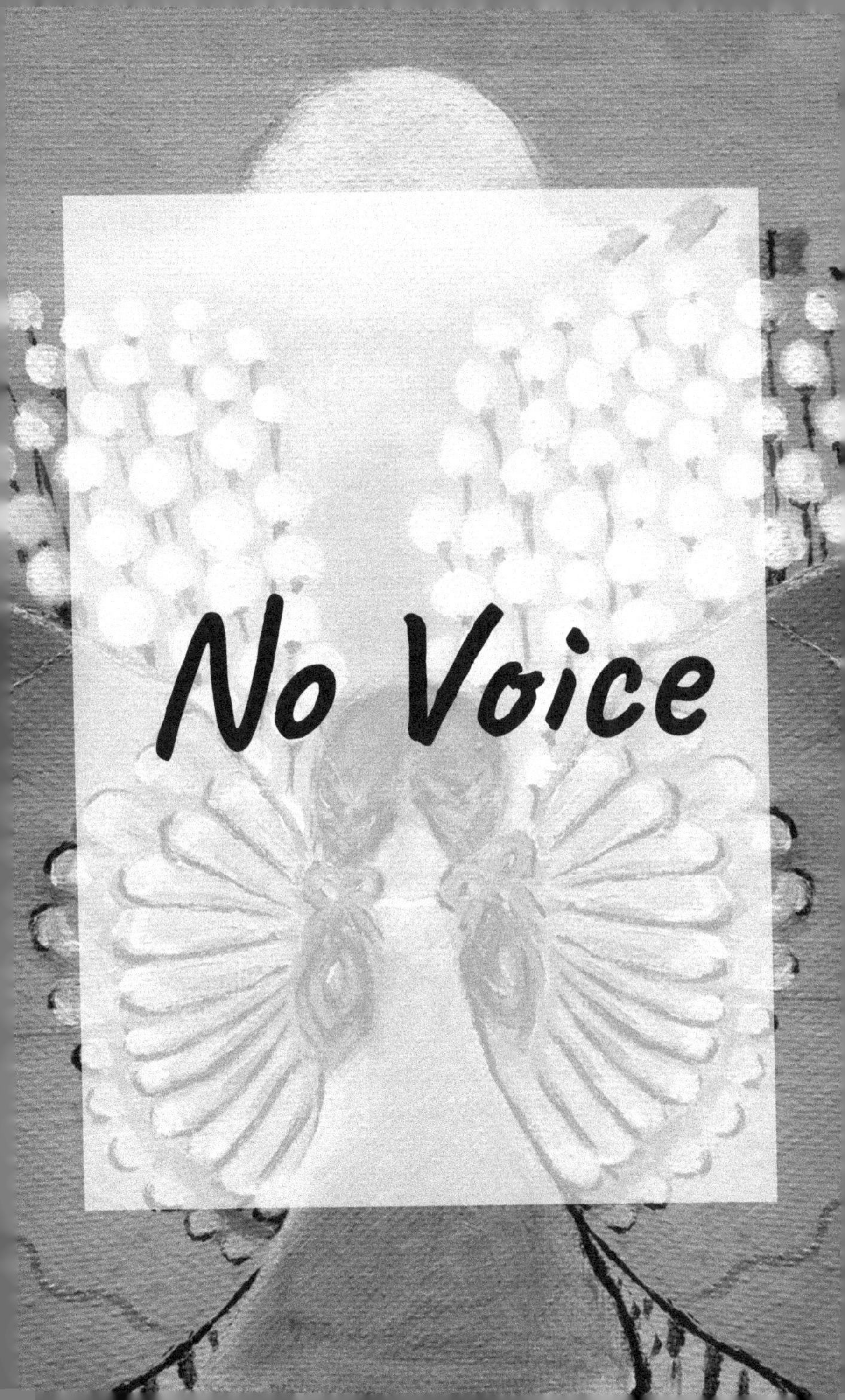
No Voice

Shhhhhh

When my parents decided to leave their life in Mexico behind, they said goodbye to every member of their family. They did not know when or IF they would see any one of them again.

The advice given to them was to be SILENT and do what you were told to ... shhhhhhhhhhhhhh.

They were dropped off on the side of a road in the middle of the night with one plastic bag, with just a change of clothes. The advice was to wait and to be SILENT and ... shhhhhhhhhhhhhh.

When they started working in this country, they were told to hold on to that job and not say a word no matter what or how they were treated and to be SILENT and ... shhhhhhhhhhhhhhh.

This "advice" is passed on from one generation to another ... shhhhhhhhhhhhhh.

Some of the smartest people we DON'T know are silent. Some of the most resilient people we DON'T know are silent. Some of the best ideas are never expressed because we are silent ... that's what millions of us are taught. Silence.

Thank you to all the amazing humans that get it. Their VOICE has value. Thank you to the ones that are learning insights directly from those that have lived it. Thank you to the humans that are allowing our stories to be told, our ideas to be shared in educational settings and in boardrooms.

By removing the FEAR of shhhhhhhhhhh, we become more human with one another. Others begin to own their own stories and do not hold back those ideas that would have been otherwise silenced. Shhhhhhhhhhhhh no more; not for you, but for others.

Work

WORK is the prize. The poorest immigrant will gladly pick your fruit or hold a mop for hours on end and will not complain. Complaining risks losing the very thing we risked our lives for. We will work for hours on end because you didn't just give us a job you gave us a new life. Smile and ask about our day and we will be loyal because you are our FAMILIA now.

Working and Not Hiding

Some dread it while there's others who would do anything to have it. Anything! This is a picture of my father. All he and mom wanted to do when they came to the United States was work. They were willing to do anything. Picking strawberries was a dream. Washing dishes was a dream. Sewing and housecleaning were dreams.

Not having the proper documentation to work made things complicated and it kept them hidden. If they landed a job, they made sure they took care of it. As a result, they put their heads down and just did what they were told, not attracting any attention to themselves. When they received their legal documents, their faces slowly lifted, and their smiles made an appearance. This was the start. They were grateful. They were happy to work. They were appreciative that they could do it without fear of deportation and the fear of having it ALL taken away. They proudly showed up to work every day. Their dreams had come true – they had made it.

The idea of making it is so different for everyone. Dad was only earning $7.75 an hour chopping up veggies and fruits for hours on end for restaurants to use for those that could afford an evening out to enjoy. In this job he didn't have insurance. He didn't earn vacation. He had to work holidays, yet he showed up with a smile and his signature leather jacket because HE COULD. No fear of deportation. Working made him happy and that was the goal from the get-go. At $7.75 an hour - he had made it.

He passed away a couple years after this picture. This was his last job in this country ... this was his last job on this earth. It was better than his dreams. He didn't hide himself anymore and he was able to be himself-leather jacket and all.

Dreams are possible.

In honor of all the humble workers out there, the ones who won't say much, the ones that unknowingly set it up for their kids to dream bigger, please be nice to all workers from all levels everywhere. Join in the fun whenever you can - BE the fun. We are blessed to have this opportunity at our jobs, on this earth. Smile often because you can ... and why not wear leather.

My Mother - The Teacher

Mom only had a sixth-grade education because she was a woman - so why more? She begged my grandparents for more schooling, but my grandfather said no because it would be a waste of money if she was going to marry soon anyways. Old school, right? She was destined to be a wife and so she married dad at 16, but she always wanted to be a teacher. She retired as a janitor from a high school a few years ago, and she tells me her favorite part was talking to the students that would take the time while she was cleaning to look up and say hello. She felt seen. I imagine her putting the mop aside and looking that child softly in the eyes, smiling and giving wise advice and ending with "keep going to school - you need EDUCATION to be better." She didn't have a classroom, but she taught kids in the halls and the stalls - mom you are a teacher.

She talked to these students about why education was good, why this country is awesome and how the simplest gestures from good people matter. Keep teaching us mom. We're all important. Let's all look up and say hello. SEE the human. We might find that the person you just made eye contact with is one of the wisest, most incredible people you'll ever meet. I love you 'Ama.

Our Normal

We don't know there are other ways until we are exposed to other things. Until then, our everyday lives, irrelevant of how we live them, are our normal.

Pig on The Street

We didn't end up in Los Angeles like a lot of my family members. My grandfather, Pancho, had been working at a soap company in Northern California as a janitor and said there was work here. Work? Off to Northern California we went. There were less Mexicans in this area than in Los Angeles. I can think of only a handful of nationalities that were here at the time but despite this, we settled in the heart of what is now Silicon Valley. Although there were a couple of large tech companies, it was nowhere near the valley it is today. There were rows of colorful gladiola flower fields, cherry trees, apricot orchards, produce farms, and factories. That's what was there for us anyways.

My grandpa had secured a one-bedroom duplex for us which at the time cost $90 a month – good for three he thought. The graffiti on the walls was quickly painted over and this became our home. A few years later, my brothers Carlos and Marko were born. The house got a little tighter, but rent was low, and no one was complaining - no one complains about making it. Years passed and on sunny days the graffiti would shine through the paint. We ignored it, and instead we focused on what the house did provide. It had walls, electricity, and even water. Our humble rented home would eventually have as many as nine family members living in it. My parents never said no to helping family.

Despite the amount of people – we did a pretty good job at laying low. What? Mexicans? Until one day, everyone knew. We all made our way to my grandpa's place. His place had more outside space than ours. Like at his farm in Mexico, he was fattening pigs that, when fat enough, would be used to celebrate special occasions.

On one of those special occasions, everyone went to his place. The festivity preparations were about to begin. To start them we needed a pig. All the males in the family were ready to get the party started. The pig was not. The pig escaped and ran through the streets of the neighborhood, screaming and squealing. Neighbors we had never seen, made their way out of their houses to see what the commotion was all about. Cars slowed down and pulled over to watch the scene unfold. Everyone was confused. All the males in the family ran after that pig, one behind the other trying to stop the meal from getting run over. My brother who was a fast runner almost caught him but tripped. I always thought my brother was fast, but that pig was faster. The pig ran over him! He felt the tiny but mighty pig feet stomp on his body. Everyone, including the pig, was squealing and screaming through the streets of Northern California. There was no way to hide us now. The Mexicans were here.

Hostess Cupcake and a Coke

My most memorable birthday didn't include piñatas or balloons. Truth is, we rarely had those types of birthdays. We had only been in this country a few years and with a new baby brother and still trying to adjust to this country – money was tight. It was late March, and the sky was gloomy, and the room was dark too. I remember sitting on the bedroom floor of our one-bedroom duplex, that now slept five, alongside my brother Carlos, my mom and my dad and my baby brother in the crib. My father had run to the little store that was located across the street. The store was literally called, "The Little Store." He brought back two packs of Hostess cupcakes and a Coke in a bottle. I loved this combo, and he knew it. Mom also ran to the kitchen to do her part; she got a match from a match box and that was my candle. I don't think I got a gift. That candle brought in a little light and brightened up the dark bedroom. I blew the match. There on the floor that day in 1978 with my family, we all enjoyed this impromptu feast. We proceeded to eat the delicious cakes all while we passed the bottle of Coca-Cola around. I kicked off five like this. I've had many birthdays of course, but this one, by far, was my most memorable one ever. Maybe it was my dad's ability to turn anything into a celebration, maybe my mom's way of adding light, maybe the simpleness of the celebration. Every year, I try to have a cupcake and coke in memory of simpler times.

The Sandwich

A day before a first-grade field trip, my mother sent me across the street for ham, bread, and chips (yes, the streets were safer then). I was perplexed, I didn't grow up eating sandwiches. I grew up eating beans, rice, and tortillas. I bought the items, brought them home, went on the field trip, and put that memory in the memory bank. Now that I am older, I realize my mother was protecting me. How? Yes, although this was subtle ... to her, being different was not a good thing, speaking Spanish equated to something negative. Being from another country was negative. Wearing non-American clothes—nope. Therefore, my lunch had to be like everyone else's so I wouldn't get teased and stand out - the sandwich helped me blend.

I reflect on this, and I am so glad I can eat my lunch no matter what it is these days and have no care in the world. Thank you, Mom, for protecting me always and I thank all of you who welcome all to the table no matter what our lunch is. P.S. I am not very good at blending.

Jumping Chickens

I remember my first interpreting experience. I was only five when my younger brothers and I had itchy red spots all over our little bodies. We scratched, we itched, but since we had no insurance, our non-English speaking momma waited until it was completely urgent to take us to the doctor. While at the hospital, the doctor turned to me and said, "Tell your mom, you have chicken pox." I paused.

What in the world is chicken pox? They didn't teach this in kinder! In my little five-year old brain I thought, chicken (pock pock pock) and pox sounded like POP (a jumping movement). So, I proudly turned to my mom and said, "Mom, we have jumping chickens!" I will never forget the look on her face.

Friends, I have been a CIO (Chief Interpreting Officer) for my family for over four decades. Many of the children who have non-English speaking families are. To this day, I am still interpreting - although I now know what chicken pox are.

My mom was scared to speak English back then, any accent could be a big red flag and have her sent back to her birth country. She was not risking that. As a result, she was silent for many years. Why a five-year old becomes an interpreter and why a mom is silent has its reasons. Don't forget, sometimes we need to laugh at the silliness that can yield some of the greatest lessons.

Tomato Hair

I was about five or six and I had the coolest natural red, auburn hair. It was unique. My mom was so proud of me and my hair. Every morning she put extra effort before she went to work to make sure it looked on point. She would make the tightest two ponytails; they were so tight my face hurt. Nothing was going to mess up my hair ... or so we thought.

To hold my hair in place mom didn't use hair spray. She used something a bit more "organic". She'd grabbed a thin cloth and wrapped half a tomato or lemon and squeezed the juice onto my head. Don't laugh, when you don't have stuff, you get very resourceful. In minutes, it dried, and voila—nature's hairspray.

You'd think nothing would mess up this perfectly styled hair. Wrong! Every day for weeks, I'd come home with messy hair - one pony tail up and one down. Mom couldn't figure it out. Until I confessed that yes, I was getting beat up on the playground. I dreaded recess.

Mom was never violent, but she sat me down one day and looked me in the eyes and said, "Do not let yourself be taken advantage of. Next time you are disrespected you let them have it." What does that mean, (Let them have it!) I first thought? Then I realized it was my GREEN LIGHT!

She should have probably been more specific because the next day during recess I didn't duck and let myself get beat up. I gave it all I had and let the kid "have it" - her hair was a mess. Her mom confronted my mom - to my mom's surprise, I proudly admitted my crime (I don't lie). Mom was so embarrassed, but secretly proud, I'd like to think. That person never messed with my perfectly, crispy red vegetable juice hair again.

There are always people who will want to see us down, people who feel better about themselves by making others feel less than, people who mistake our niceness for weakness, people who feel powerFUL by making others feel powerLESS. This is wrong. We should all know that their mean is not a reflection of us - it's all them. Sadly, I've met people like this my whole life—5 or 45.

It's up to us to put a stop to it! SAY SOMETHING!

We should all have limits. We should all have boundaries, but we're not born knowing how to recognize when or how to deal with them. We need to be taught that sometimes enough is enough. Thank you, Mom, for giving me the courage to stand up for myself even if I did go a little overboard that one time.

May we all have the strength to speak up and say, "No more."

A Branch and a Can

I grew up humbly, but it wasn't until I was older that I realized I was poor. Before that, it was just life. It was all I knew. For the most part, my parents did everything in their power not to bring attention to what we didn't have. As years passed, I think back to my holidays growing up. We never had a real, out-of-the lot Christmas tree. There was even a year that mom cut a tip of the branch from the pine tree outside and put it in a coffee can, and just like that-instant Christmas. Our gifts were humble. My brother asked for a baseball bat one year and mom not knowing any better got him a red plastic one. To this day he still remembers and cries, but he's never said a word to mom-that's not important. My parents did what they could and although some Christmases were "coffee can" Christmases, we have always done one thing consistently-if we can, we get together. We all head to mom's house on December 24th to indulge and unwrap homemade tamales, her gift to us yearly, and that tops any baseball bat we could ask for.

I have a beautiful large tree in my front window these days, plenty of gifts, but I have never forgotten those Christmases when a branch and a can were more than enough. Whatever you celebrate, whatever you eat, remember what's important and enjoy and savor it.

Toby the Invisible Man

Toby would walk our small town when we were kids – he had no house. He had a calm, steady walk, he never said anything, and never made eye contact. He slept under the cement bridge by our house, and he didn't bother anyone, and we didn't bother him. I never saw him get drunk, beg for food or money; we just left him alone and he left us alone. Although we saw him, he was invisible.

One day, on one of his walks, with a safe distance- he extended out his right hand and in it was a clear plastic bag containing 4 of the largest, reddest, shiniest apples we had ever seen. We took them and ran home to tell mom. To this day my brothers and I remember this moment. It confused us because he was giving US something, not the reverse. This was a symbol of peace. With four apples, an unhoused man made himself VISIBLE that day. An "I exist" moment. Toby was no longer an invisible man but a quiet human with no home. Years passed and he continued to walk our little town, each year slower and slower while we were faster and faster. Although we never spoke to him, we no longer avoided eye contact. We waved when we saw him, and he waved back and that was that. Apples? Who would have thought.

VISIBILITY, what a great gift.

"Bowling" in Style

My father used to take us to three places religiously on Sundays: The Flea Market, Thrifty's (for a 15-cent scoop of ice cream), and the bowling alley. I want to tell you a story about number three today. I remember the first-time dad said, "Let's go there," (in Spanish). My brothers and I were shocked. We didn't grow up with "sports" in our family aside from the Saturday night Lucha libre matches, so for him to take us to a bowling alley was a big deal. I am not even sure how he knew about it.

I remember walking in for the first time, not knowing what to expect. Do we play? How do we play? It smelled funny. The shoes were silly, but we just let dad guide us. We felt the stares. Our church attire didn't fit in with the casual attire worn in the alley, but we kept walking in. He proceeded to put a bill in a coin machine and gave me and my brothers some quarters. This was the 80's so Pac-Mac and Air Hockey were a big thing! We played non-bowling games until the quarters ran out. Never did we go up to a counter and play a real bowling game. For an hour or two, we didn't care about our clothes or the stares. We just played.

Although many would say this type of outing was not ideal, that our clothing was not ideal. Looking back, it was ideal for US. As I've gotten older, I've come to realize that different situations work for different people, and no one should judge. You never know what anyone's situation is or why. Dad was just looking to mix up the activities he did with his kids.

He knew nothing about bowling shoes, strikes, or spares. All he knew was he had a couple spare hours on Sunday after church and that if he placed a bill in a machine, his kids would have a little fun. Thank you, Dad, for taking us out on Sundays, for the flea market trips, the scoop of ice cream, and for leaving a memory in my mind that makes me view bowling alleys and families in fancy clothing completely different. The arcade was OUR sport, Pac-Man was OUR game, and Air Hockey was OUR thing and wow, did we look good playing them. It worked for US, period.

I drove by the spot that used to be that bowling alley the other day on the way back from dad's grave. The bowling alley was gone. This month dad will be gone 29 years too. If dad would have cared what others thought of us going in the bowling alley, I would've never had these memories. Never worry about what others might say or might think. If it feels good, keep "walking in," and ignore the stares and comments. If it works for you and yours, that's good enough. DO IT and do it often.

Everything in life is temporary. Jobs, Lucha libre fights, arcades, bowling games, ice cream, and yes, even our parents. Enjoy them all while they're present. Appreciate the time because we never know when the machine of life runs out of quarters.

Bus 26

Immigrating into a new country is hard: New food, new language, new customs. Dad was used to women doing "old school" wife things in Mexico, and he was comfortable with that here too. It's what he knew. It wasn't his fault. Mom was alright with it too until one day she just wasn't.

She asked dad to take us to the store to get us out of the house and he said no. She said nothing but it ate her up. Was she just going to sit there and have to ask every time hoping for him to say yes? NO! That week mom started her research, asking neighbors this and that. The weekend came, she got us kids ready, we held hands, walked to the bus-stop, and waited for bus 26.

The 26 arrived, the doors opened outward as if welcoming us in (insert angelic sound here ahhh). The bus driver smiled, mom put a few coins in that coin thing and off we went. That easy? She didn't have to stay in the house? She didn't need to ask for permission? She could see new things and new places. She just needed to take the first step and want it, research a little, and boom! She could make her own yes! Bus 26 was freedom. She never "hoped" for a yes again and dad let his butterfly be.

Garbage Bag Raincoat

When you don't know any other way, it just is. No wonder others that knew other ways looked at me "sideways." Sideways was my normal. As kids, mom walked us to the bus stop at the end of our street. You'd think we were walking from one side of the world to another. Our side, falling down homes, no insulation. But over by the bus stop, there were houses with fancy doorbells and heaters.

One morning before school, a big rainstorm hit. How were we going to get to the other side? My quick-thinking mama grabbed black garbage bags, cut a small hole for our head and arm holes and we made the trek. We didn't think anything of it except we were dry. I got on the bus and immediately sensed whispers and felt stares. The bus driver yelled "SILENCE!!!" and off we went. I had no idea what I wore labeled me.

I've weathered hard rains, but I didn't do it alone. I am grateful for the beautiful humans that shielded me from storms, negative whispers, labels, and those who helped get me to the other side. I AM HERE because of you. Let's not use our raincoat type as a judge for anyone. We don't know the whole story sometimes. Consider the sun, after all, don't we all end up on the school bus of life together anyways? With a raincoat or not?

Golden Teardrops

 When I was seven or eight, Mom worked in a flower nursery making a couple dollars an hour. In our family culture, it was tradition to buy your daughter gold jewelry when you felt successful and were able. At the flower nursery mom cut thorns off roses and dead petals from flowers. At the time, we had no legal status. We were sharing our one bedroom rented home with a half-dozen people. She spoke no English, yet my mother felt successful.

She saved about $50 to buy me these earrings four decades ago; they're called Golden Teardrops. What a beautiful name and honestly a great metaphor for the life of anyone working hard to make it. I rarely wore them as a young person because I didn't get it. Now I wear them often in honor of her sacrifice. How many times did those thorns cut her for her to save enough? I can't imagine. Success can be so simple. If you ever see a little girl with gold bling, know there's a proud momma feeling successful behind her—a momma that was able.

I proudly wore these earrings the first time I spoke about my journey. She saw them on me on a stage-the flower money had paid off. Success-what a beautiful feeling. Yes, success is a feeling! A feeling of being able.

Free Cheese

As an undocumented family growing up, we had no access to help; we knew that. With our $90 a month rent and $60 monthly expenses, my parents hustled to work anywhere making minimum wage to help pay what was needed to live. Occasionally, we'd have a little extra and head to Goodwill to splurge. And if we were lucky, for 25 cents, we'd get a small plastic bag full of old hand me down toys. The highlight of the trip!

For food, my mother was creative, and nothing was wasted. I still could smell the fresh tomatoes she grew in any patch of dirt she could find. Now and then, the local schools would make announcements offering free cheese with no question on legal status. What? Free cheese? No questions? Yeah! It was a 5-pound block of yellowness that to us felt like a block of gold.

For weeks mom's creativity was exhibited on the kitchen table: Cheese enchiladas, cheese potato tacos, "chilaquiles" with cheese, cheese anything and cheese everything.

Gratefully, no one was lactose intolerant. To this day, I have a love for yellow cheese and an appreciation for parents that do what they must. To turn a block of yellow nothing into an experience that means everything is pure magic. Thank you, Mom, for not letting us feel our "status", but most of all for letting us taste our freedom over and over.

Slow and Steady - Not Always

When I was a little girl, we went to a festival. It was one of these "potato sack" type of events where there's tons of kid games. One of the games was a race of some sorts. All the kids were to line up, side by side, with a plastic spoon, handle side in mouth, with the spoon side holding a bean. Whoever got to the finish line without dropping the bean first won. I was an extremely fast sprinter, and so I thought for sure I had this game won!

The announcer yelled, "On your marks, get set, GO!" In that moment my sprinting abilities went out the window and my perfectionist trait made its presence. UGH!! I went, but instead of using my legs to run as fast as I could, I headed to the end very slowly. I wasn't going to drop the bean for anything. That wasn't the real point of this game though. All of us could have made it to the finish line without dropping the bean (eventually) but only a few of us could have used our running skills to have a better chance of winning. I had a chance and didn't go for it.

I learned that slow and steady does sometimes win the race. BUT there are times where just GOING FOR IT, using what we have and not looking back is absolutely the right strategy. No overthinking—just GO! In our quest to have everything right, everything checked, everything perfect, we may actually end up behind and miss opportunities. Those in competition with you might be the ones that are just going for it.

Age is but a Number

My father was orphaned at eight and never had a bike, but he taught me how to ride one though. It was a $10 rusted old bike from the flea market. I could barely sit as it was too big for my body and it creaked, but it didn't matter. He held the back of the big seat while I peddled and when the wobbling stopped, he let go; I was ready. He was so proud.

One day, he got enough courage to ask me to teach him to ride. I was about 11; he was 36. The bike was getting rustier by the minute, and it still creaked, but it was the perfect height for him. We set up in the middle of the street; I held the back of the big seat, he peddled, the wobbling stopped, and I let go—he was ready. I was so proud.

His birthday was coming up and I wanted to surprise him. I had saved some paper route money. I still remember the feeling of setting it up outside the door. He could not believe this NEW, red, shiny bike in front of him was his. He exuded a childlike happiness that day. He rode that bike everywhere, chin up, and proud.

He's been gone a long time, but this memory lives in my wobbly mind, and I can't let it go. Remember the small things; always; remember to teach. Neither of us were conventional learners or teachers. He didn't let my young age be a roadblock, and I wasn't blocked because he was older. Humans for humans. Period.

EGGxactly

I've always loved science but sadly due to lack of resources could never participate in science fairs.

I knew when the teacher mentioned the science fair, that it wasn't for me. I couldn't exactly run to the art and craft store, or Michael's, for poster board and markers, and I definitely didn't have the means to create an exploding volcano.

However, one day the science teacher asked everyone to come up with a way to drop an egg from the school roof without wrapping it in clothing; you could only use supplies you had at home. The person whose egg survived won!

Oh boy! I had nothing at home. We had no garage with supplies. No fancy supply box. Now what? Was this not for me too? I was about 10 at the time and had a newspaper route. When it would rain, I'd have to put the newspapers in plastic bags. The bags were the only extra supply I had, and it wasn't raining! Hallelujah. Here's what I did: I blew up about three or four long bags and tied the ends. I positioned the egg between all the bags and wrapped the tape tightly around the bags. That's it. It gave the egg protection, and with the blown-up bags, I figured that it should provide enough bounce to keep it whole (or at least that was my hope).

It was contest day. I saw everyone's egg concoctions. Come on ... egg on a parachute! I knew many went out and bought fancy supplies.

The contest began and the egg projects began to drop from the school roof. One broke, then two, three, and so on. What a mess the contest had made already.

It was my turn. The teacher had never seen a newspaper bag concoction. I took a deep breath and when the plastic protected egg dropped, guess what? It did not break!

I never entered a science fair, but I did win the science contest that day, with just some plastic bags and tape. Who would've thought? Sometimes those with the least number of resources are forced to get incredibly creative. Our way of solving problems might be unlike something you've ever seen. Maybe it's just what you need. Being resourceful is an everyday practice for us. This skill for me has been huge in my professional career. When budgets are tight; when we have to do a lot with a little, I got this. When considering talent, consider the value of those coming from underserved places; those that were forced to get it done somehow.

The egg type projects won't appear on a resume, but know it will show up in their work and it might even exceed your EGGspectations.

The Flyer

Remember when you were a kid and you brought home flyers for soccer, music, and track? I do, but with parents who barely made minimum wage, I learned fast that those flyers were not for us and into the trash they went; time and time again. Even though I ran faster than most kids, I couldn't run track or play soccer. I loved music, but never could join a class. I just knew to throw away the flyers. Except once.

A bright yellow flyer with black letters that read: "After-School Art Classes $20." I did a double take on the cost- $20 dollars; I still questioned it. Surely, we could scrape that up, right? I begged and begged and after a lot of begging, I was shocked that mom finally said yes. It was happening! I was going to be able to stay after school like a "normal" kid for once! I drew this and drew that, then the class ended. The instructor asked us to not forget to bring another $20 the next week. Wait, what?

Another $20?

I just knew my artistic days had come to an end with just ONE class. I was "normal" for just once, I thought as I threw away the flyers for the rest of my school years. Underserved does not mean we can't, it just means we couldn't. Thank you to all of you who seek to understand our perspective, those that help, those that listen, and those that let us feel what it's like to not crumple the flyer ... ONCE.

Off to Work

In a world where so many grumble and complain about having to get up and go to work; a world where it's normalized to have excuses, there are people that happily wake up everyday much earlier than dawn to work. They make breakfast and lunch for the day, get their kids dressed for school—even if they have to tuck them back in—and maybe, if they are lucky, they have a cup of coffee. They leave their home with the moon and stars still shining to make the dream of work a reality. They do this for years because that's what they came to this country to do ... work—no matter if it's in the dark. Dark doesn't scare us, it motivates us.

I'm a Girl?

For me, being a female has not been an issue or perhaps the fact that it was never brought to my attention helped. Here's a little story. When I was ten, I was asked by a neighborhood boy if I could take over his newspaper route. This was the 80's so getting the news via actual paper and getting it delivered on the porch was VIP service. There was no Google back then, but I wanted to deliver the news. I wanted to be Google! The job entailed folding 40 newspapers (which would cause you to have semi-permanent black ink marks on your fingertips), packing them in the old school handlebar bags and delivering them rain or shine, every single day afterschool.

Earnings would be $40 per month/$1 per paper. I imagined all the candy bars and ice-cream I'd buy with the money. I wanted it so bad! I wanted dollars so bad. I wanted ice-cream so bad. My parents and I didn't know that 99% of the kids that typically did this job were boys. The boy recruiting me didn't care either. This was an all-boy industry and there I was, raising my hand, begging. My parents were hesitant because every day seemed like a lot for a ten-year old.

My counter was I'd have money every day, weekends, and holidays—something I lacked daily. My parents agreed to let me try. I loved it. Within months, I was adding more and more newspaper subscriptions to my route and every year for four years a NEW SHINY "BOYS" BMX BIKE would appear on our doorstep as a prize for being a top newspaper carrier. Me—the one percent. I had three large routes by age 14. Morning, evening, and doubled up on Wednesdays, delivering news, coupons, and store ads everywhere. To get to everyone, I had my brothers work for me and I gave them a bike as an incentive. I was a girl in a boy's world, and I wasn't scared because neither my parents nor I knew any better. Being good was not a boy or a girl thing. It was a work hard thing.

Ignorance is bliss sometimes. If obstacles are invisible and unsaid, sometimes we just pass right through them. I am proof that the less that is spoken about the I can'ts ... the more we might actually do.

Trailer Park Lessons

I'd like to say I was in the subscription business before it was a thing. What kind of lesson could I possibly learn from delivering papers to older people in a trailer park? Read on.

It didn't take long to figure out that if I delivered the paper on the porch and spent a few minutes listening to these folks' stories, I'd get a dollar tip at the end of the month. Why was this so important? At first, for me at 10 years old, a dollar meant five, 19-cent ice cream bars (yes, I ate them all.) For them, it was about a human that listened and made it easier for their aging body to get the news faster, their connection to the outside world. I helped make that easier. Yep, just like Google.

Month after month, I knocked on their trailers collecting the monthly dues. At first, I'd brace myself as I knew I'd need to spend a few extra minutes listening to stories of their cats, their kids, their memories of the past. But wait, after a while, I looked forward to knocking on their door. I didn't know why. Was it the dollar, the ice cream? I was too young to realize it was the gift of their stories. Their faces would light up for a few minutes as I listened to stories about living. I liked seeing their faces light up. Stories were a confirmation that it happened. Listening was a confirmation someone cared.

The many years I spent as a kid collecting subscription dues and listening to stories have paid off decades later. I learned that everything is a lesson in this life. I learned the lessons of patience, listening, and the valuable lesson of TIME. RIP my trailer park storytellers.

As you sit with your family and friends, don't just sit there, ask them questions. Listen with patience. You are making someone's day by staying still and allowing them to feel alive through memories. If your family is hard to talk to, I dare you to just sit with them and ask them what, why, and how questions. Ask them to explain memories and details to you. You might be surprised what comes back and the very act of you expressing interest might just be what that person needed to feel alive. To feel alive—what a beautiful gift. Universe— it was never about the ice cream sandwiches, was it? Lesson learned.

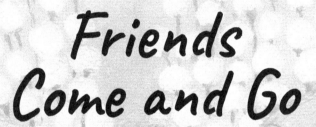

Friends Come and Go

Everyone is put in your path for a reason but not everyone is meant to stay in your life forever. Sometimes you outgrow people, differences arise, or you simply move or move on. This is life. Whatever the case, everyone carries a message, a lesson for you. Everyone.

Mac-N-Cheese for Tamales

Growing up, I was a tomboy. Afterall, I grew up with all boys. There were no girls in my neighborhood. Until one day, this pretty girl named Denise with blue eyes showed up - finally someone who didn't want to wrestle! She lived in the one-bedroom duplex on the other side of me. It was the perfect setup for instant friends. For a couple years she and I were inseparable.

I used to go to her house for mac-n-cheese and she'd come to mine for Mexican food. I remember her biting into a tamale once and she said, "chewy" because she didn't know she was supposed to take OFF the husk. That's how it went for a couple years. She showed me MTV and I showed her piñatas. Although she and I looked completely different, our living situations were identical. We both were living in one-bedroom homes with a lot of people. We both needed space. Our siblings were too annoying for our "cool" tween selves.

Being tweens, we wanted privacy. How do you make privacy out of nothing though? Our parents put their creativity to work and in no time at all, the washing machine was moved outside, and we moved into the laundry room. One problem, the mattresses were too long for the space. What problem? In true "we will figure it out" mode ... with a saw and a steady hand, about a half foot of mattress made its way to the trash. The new-sized mattress fit perfectly in our new bedroom, and we were short in stature, so we fit perfectly too. With a curtain hanging on the wall opening of the old laundry room— we had privacy for the first time in our lives.

Adversity brought us together. Although she had blue eyes and lighter skin, she was going through the same things I was. Our ability to share our differences also brought us together. Her and her mac-n-cheese, and me and my tamales (with the HUSKS OFF).

There are places in this world where color is not the only diversity factor. Consider adversity. Consider the story. You might find that we are more alike than different.

Fitting In

I was in junior high when I was passed a note in math class that read, "We don't want you around us." I was heartbroken. The friends I once considered my equals now looked like movie stars and my cute, little girl appearance now seemed "distorted." I had acne, a funky haircut, and hand-me-down clothes. How was I supposed to compete? Well, I didn't. What then?

I feared lunch time. I built up my courage every day to see if any group would want a new lunch friend. NO from the jocks, NO from the artsy kids, NO from my old classmates. Oh, one YES from the stoners but probably not the best idea. I spent about a year lonely, trying to fit in.

This time in our lives is hard and it too shall pass. Fast forward. You will be ok. Our time comes when it's meant to come. There will be a lot of no's, but don't give up hope. You will find your people. Yes, people who once passed on us might one day wish they would have shared a sandwich with US.

Free Donuts – I'm In!

I only knew what I saw. You know when you are asked at school what you want to be when you grow up? I remember struggling to answer this question. I didn't know. I only knew what I saw at home and what I saw on TV. The TV jobs like "General Hospital" seemed unattainable, and at home, mom was at a factory and dad was getting home with muddy boots daily. This is a hard question when the options seem minimal—we need to be shown as many "REAL", attainable options as possible and shown how to get them.

Beth

I am the first in my family to be in an office. I remember the first time I was allowed into an office for a reason other than to clean it. I was 14 and working in the warehouse with my mom, and like all moms, she tried to cover my errors. After a while, it was obvious, I sucked at doing warehouse work. However, the owner didn't get mad. Instead, she sat me down and gave me another option. She said, "Honey, come on over this way," and with her hand on my shoulder, she opened the door to a setting my family had never seen. I was in an office.

She opened the door. Another option? Yes, I had another option, and the owner knew it. Her name was Beth. Turns out not being good at warehouse work was a blessing in disguise. It opened my eyes to a clean environment (aside from the cigarette ashes on the desk, because after all it was the 80's). There were drinks in a fridge, donuts on the table, and I didn't have to wait for a specific breaktime to have any of it.

My hands were clean and unlike my amazing warehouse friends and even my mother, I had a heater. It was hard to NOT feel guilty. My mother was proud. Every time I'd walk to the back to say hi, her face lit up. I was just a teen and getting paid $3.35 an hour. But, in her eyes, I had "made it". I guess I could have stopped there, but Beth kept teaching me. Telling me to take typing classes. Showing me how to do things. She was patient.

Beth opened my eyes to a new world because she saw that I could do something else. I liked that she liked me. I liked that she told me with words. Speaking was hard in my family, so Beth unknowingly filled this gap. It wasn't my parents' fault, they only knew what they knew. But Beth knew other things and she believed in me. She was my first work believer, and I worked for her during most of my teenage years. I had perfected work, and at 14 had accomplished more than my parents. I had achieved my parents dream of WORK and working in an office was the ultimate prize.

Beth could not have been more different than me with her white pearls and I in my three-dollar shoes and four-inch-high hair, but it didn't matter to either of us. I helped her achieve her goals and well, she helped me realize that I needed to raise mine. Let's appreciate our believers and open doors often. And if you have never entered an office, just know it could change the course of your life. It did for me. Let's all be Beths and be Beths for others.

And This is Why

Living in the humblest of homes in the United States is nothing like living in the humblest homes in other countries. For some, having the basics like water, electricity and even a bathroom is already better. Many live in these humble places where despite the lack of resources, they remain hopeful that one day they will see their loved one—even if it's in the dark.

Vacation In Mexico – First Time Back

After over a dozen years of waiting for legal documents – it finally happened, we received our green card! No more hiding. We had heard endless stories about "back home", but we really didn't get it, until we got there.

There was no water, no electricity, no gas, no real walls, the floor was dirt. Worse, no place to plug in my curling iron! My brother made a toilet out of a few stacked tires just so that he'd have a place to sit.

However, since a dozen years had passed, this home had more than many around had. By this time the money my grandfather had earned being a janitor in the United States had started seeing its impact too. My aunts who lived there were studying. There was land with vegetables and fruits all around. There was hope that they, too, would soon leave for a better place in the town nearby— and they did. They left for better too.

The visit was insightful, and we were glad to get on a plane and come back without questions. I wondered what my parents thought that first time back from Mexico when their passport was stamped?

Please consider WHY people might risk everything. A risk is a chance, and a chance is always worth taking.

I know for some the United States is not perfect, but for me and millions, it's home.

I never again take for granted the luxury of plugging in anything and just having it work.

High School – No Bueno

While some did cheer and played tennis after school, I rushed to get on the bus everyday to get to work. I had to. I had no idea WHY high school was important. No one in my family had finished junior high much less high school. They worked and that's what I did.

Drama

At one point, I was failing everything in high school. I had to work and honestly, I didn't get why education was so important. No one had ever taught my parents about the educational system. I tell you, had they been obligated to learn the basics of this country's educational system at the time they applied for a green card, they gladly would have learned it. A green card for an immigrant is the ultimate prize. Perhaps, education and immigration should go hand in hand? It would have saved me a ton of stress too.

My parents didn't even know that in the United States there are four years of high school because in Mexico there are three. They didn't know the grading system. At first, they didn't even know that an "F" was not fantastico. They didn't know that pushing for college as early as possible could be the best investment they could ever make. No one showed them, so they didn't show me. I wish my parents knew more.

I went to school, but that was not my focus. I worked as often as possible, just like them. We needed to bring in money and we needed it now, so I did. I was good at work. I helped to pay bills and rent because SURVIVAL was important. These years were confusing. Despite my tough exterior, inside, I felt like a loser. I felt the eye rolls when I entered a classroom. Once I was even accused of cheating because I got the highest grade on a science test. The truth was I had a natural interest in science and enjoyed it, and besides, I was not a cheater. But the negativity demoralized me.

I was getting encouraged at work, but I didn't have much encouragement in school except by one person—my drama teacher. Despite the fact that I was failing his class, he worked with me. It must have been hard to have me as a student. I was disengaged, tired and because I had to work after school; I could never make practices.

For my final, instead of a group project, the drama teacher asked me to memorize a monologue. No group project? That, I could do. It didn't require me to stay after school and I could learn it on my breaks at work.

But why learn it? I was failing the class. I couldn't explain it at the time, but I wanted to prove that I could do THIS. Maybe to my teacher, maybe to myself, so I practiced when I could.

The day of the final came, and I went on that school stage knowing I would fail the class regardless, but I did it anyway. I left everything on the stage that day. Everything. I didn't know what to expect. Oh, an F, I thought to myself. It was something bigger than a grade though. I think the teacher knew this too. At the end of the monologue the teacher stood up, I think his eyes even watered, and I can still remember it now—him clapping almost in slow motion. He was the only one in the class that stood up that day. That was enough. I did it.

For decades, I have been trying to rack my brain for the name of that one teacher; that on that day of a final, who looked at me with pride and stood up for me—clap, clap.

Time passed.

My love for the stage grew over the years. I admired speakers, performers, and motivators. Eventually, I even became a backstage mom for my kids. I never could quite make it on a stage though. Until 30 years later. I immediately was that high school kid that wanted to prove that I could. I did. If I could only tell that teacher.

I recently came across an article from 1990 with a picture of that drama teacher. Under it, the name: Mr. Burkhart. Immediately after finding his name, I found his obituary. I hope he knew ...

This teacher was the only ONE in high school that ever stood up for me ... and he did it alone.

Once might be all we need.

To all the Mr.Burkhart's out there, thank you.

Don't Assume

The teacher had just passed back our graded science tests. I've always found the sciences fascinating. Instead of the teacher passing the test to each individual, he had the front row student pass them back. The test scores were not a secret. As I got my test handed to me, I noticed a big A+. I had the highest grade in the class. I was proud for a half second-literally just a half a second when the person next to me whispered "How'd you cheat?" I replied, "I didn't."

He didn't believe me, and I think even the teacher believed I cheated too. You see, I was part of the minority in my school. People who looked like me, who dressed like me, were stereotyped. To some, we were the losers, the gang members, the cheaters. I must be honest, as a teen I thought maybe I'm NOT supposed to get A's or like science-maybe I'm supposed to be "that" stereotype. What was I doing getting an A+ in science? Well, I loved science. I had studied between classes, afterschool, work breaks, so I was bound to get an A.

There will always be non-believers who can't be happy for you, and some are right next to us. We can't let them bring us down. Their assumptions cannot define us. Prove them wrong. Prove YOU right.

"You're a Bad Influence"

I was the kid in high school who was called a bad influence by the principal. I guess I looked a little scary with my four-inch-high hair ... but bad? Regardless, he kicked me out. He never asked me why I couldn't come to class on time. I was working nights to help my parents, because my father was dying of cancer, and I had to help.

I ended up at a continuation school, and it turned out that the other kids there were also in bad situations like me. Some were 14-year-old parents, some were pregnant, some were homeless, some were abused, some had drug issues, some had parents with drug issues, some had no parents, but in all the situations it was not their fault. No one asked them why or what happened? We were all a product of our environment. We all wore the same inexpensive clothes, six-dollar sweatshirts, and three-dollar Mary Jane shoes from the Flea Market, and no one would tease other people or other groups. Our tough exterior was our protection from the pain, but we were too young to understand that or even articulate it.

One day, a counselor at that continuation school sat me down and was relentless in asking me WHY. At first, I was stubborn in telling him the truth. That is, until it just came out and I told him. I was working, my father was dying, and I needed to help.

In that moment he realized I was not a bad kid at all. I was just in a mess, and I was dealing with heavy issues. Instead of brushing me off, here's what he did. He took the time and wrote me a plan to get out of that school. So that I could graduate on time. That plan to me was my HOPE plan and all because he was relentless in asking WHY.

Three letters changed my path in life. W-H-Y. None of us kids at that school were bad; we all were just in bad situations, but I was able to get out because someone took the time to help me, which in-turn, gave me something to hang onto—hope. Having hope in what seems like a hopeless situation is priceless.

My name is Martha, I proudly represent the two percent of Latinas in tech. I've been doing it for over 25 years— we need more. I've been in hardware, software, and mobile. I broke the cycle of poverty, but I didn't do it alone. It took good people (like the counselor at that school) and employers that gave an opportunity to someone different,

even though I was that someone with three-dollar Mary Jane shoes. These people saw beyond my scary, four-inch-high hair.

Let's do more of that.

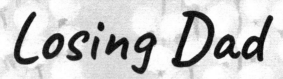

Losing Dad

My father died of cancer at only 44 years of age. I think about loss and grief often and why it hurts so much. It's the fact that we saw that person in our future and when they are not—it's impossible not to hurt.

Thanksgiving

Thanksgiving is mom's favorite holiday. Why? It's simple. To us, it's a day of appreciation of everything good in our lives. When she came to the United States, she had no clue what it was, but over time she slowly caught on. In the early nineties she missed it, my father had been diagnosed with cancer, and she was in Mexico. Why? She had seen a TV news report about "healing" water from a remote well in a tiny town and she couldn't stop thinking about it, so she bought a ticket to Mexico as soon as she could and left to find the magic well. When she arrived at the small town, she bought an overpriced, 5-gallon container and proceeded on the long walk to fill it with this water. That year, my kid brothers and I cooked and ate a flavorless turkey and hoped mom would get back soon with the cure for dad. When she got back, he drank the water daily with HOPE until the last drop. I can't imagine how desperate they were to even do this.

I thank the universe for all those who hope, execute, and although sometimes fail, it doesn't matter, because no one can say they didn't try.

A Hospice Story

My brothers and I were teenagers when we lost dad. He was only 42 when he was diagnosed with esophageal cancer, even though he rarely smoked. Mom kept the diagnosis from us for a bit and tried to stay strong, but we knew something was wrong when dad was home, getting thinner by the day, and she had to take on a second job. Everyday mom had to be stronger while dad got weaker.

This went on for two years until he was hospitalized. They registered him in a room on the hospice floor. On one of our visits, in the hospital parking lot, a lady asked me and my brothers why we were there. We casually said, "We are visiting our dad." We all made casual chit-chat and made our way into the hospital elevator. When she asked what floor we were on, so she could press the button for us- she froze. We said he's on the hospice floor. We could tell something was wrong. She lowered her eyes and slowly pressed the elevator button. Awkward silence.

You see, no one had ever taught us the word HOSPICE-no one! I don't even think mom knew or perhaps she didn't want to know or maybe she was holding onto a miracle.

For one month the hospice lobby was our home. I am sure the nurses were entertained. Our family brought tacos, pizza, and pastries. As the month went by, the visits became less and less, and so did dad's strength. Less food in the lobby too. My father had lost his sense of knowing as well. He had so much medicine in his system, and I could tell he wanted to say something with his chapped dry lips, but he just couldn't get any words out. I grabbed a moist sponge and moistened his lips, as if that sponge would help the words come out, the lips that once taught me the melody to the first song I remember learning. There was nothing. No words.

On one quiet night, while mom and a couple others prayed in his room—it happened. Mom ran into the visitor's lobby of the hospice floor and woke me up and said two words "mija ya," daughter now. I knew.

I ran to his room. I cried and held his once strong hands. I could feel his bones. From the corner of his eye, a tear dripped down his sunken cheek, almost in slow motion. His expression was left like he wanted to say something. I needed a larger sponge! One tear, maybe he knew too and just like that, I lost my father.

LOSS is a horrible thing. Later, I found out dad was only supposed to be in hospice for a couple of days. Maybe we did get a small miracle after all. Tell others to hug and love, even if it's in an elevator. Tell those you love just that—that you love them; tell them NOW and while you still can. Tell them while you have a voice because we never know when that voice will be taken from us.

In memory of my Apa Juan and in reflection of my strong Ama Tomasa.

El Bigotes / Mr. Mustache

It was no ordinary mustache. It was RED but his hair was black, so it was unique—he was unique. He was happy, confident and his red mustache seemed to amplify his swag. How? Dad was an orphan, endured abuse, poverty, and racism. I wondered how someone who had it so bad could be so happy, have so many friends, and become a man who was so loved.

When he died at 44, I remember heading to the cemetery and looking back at the endless number of cars behind us. You would have thought it was a famous person. The line went on and on. It's interesting, he died earning less than eight dollars an hour. I knew then it wasn't about the money. It's been decades and my dad's friends still are in contact with us; they are family. Whatever he did in life, mattered.

What did he do? He offered a plate to the hungry. He offered a blanket to the cold. He sang with the lonely, laughed with the sad, gave advice to the young, never showed up empty handed, danced with the elderly, and the list goes on. He did simple things that mattered. Dad taught me that we have two options: One, let our past control us or two, move forward. In the end, we end up the same, the rich and the poor alike, right next to each other. There's no money value on a tombstone. Do good. Be kind. Let go and live forward. Love is not complex or fancy—it's a laugh, a meal, a song, a gesture, but a cool red mustache to add swag—is priceless.

Not Two Left Feet

I was talking with a friend about life and death. Both are tough subjects. She mentioned how her mom was buried with a blanket because she was always cold; this was HER thing. I completely understood.

It got me thinking about a situation that happened when I was arranging for my father's services. I decided on an open viewing. Services involved making decisions on makeup, clothes, even shoes—a lot for a teen. I bought my dad his last outfit along with his nice new shoes and I dropped them off.

The morning of, I got a call, "Sorry to bother you, but you brought us two LEFT shoes, we can put them on him, no one will know. Good?" What? Wait. Two left shoes? What should I do? I began thinking. My father was the best dancer I knew. At any party, he was the first to dance. He had anything but two left feet. I know this sounds silly, but I imagined him having these left shoes, dancing uncomfortably because of me.

NOOOOO!! NOT good! No one else would know but I knew, and I couldn't. That was it! I rushed to pick up the two left shoes and made the shoe exchange. There are things in life we cannot do retakes on; do the right thing. In my friend's mom's case, a blanket to keep her mom warm, and in my dad's case, NOT two left shoes.

Dance comfortably dad and to my friend's mom-be warm.

Dad Regrets and Caesar Salad

I had just finished high school which also meant I could now work full-time. What college? I knew that I needed to help pay bills right away. With more hours on hand, the company I had been part-timing at for years asked me to represent them at the San Francisco Giftmart. I would have to take the train for an hour, but it didn't matter. I would be able to wear high heels, a suit jacket, and possibly even carry a briefcase. I said yes immediately!

The Giftmart was a large building in central SF with permanent spaces where different manufacturers presented their product. Think of it like a big Amazon but in real life! Instead of "Google-ing it", in "the old days, if you were "searching" for vases you walked to the elevator, pressed floor X, and walked to space XX (you get the idea). Buyers from big department stores, like Mervyn's and Sears, would come by your space and see if the product you represented warranted an order for their multiple stores. If they thought it did, the order was processed in writing and on three color carbon paper. Seriously!

I worked weekends at the Giftmart too, but I didn't mind. It had a fantastic cafeteria, where they sold the best Caesar salad, hand shaved parmesan and all! I only knew of this lettuce because of my father's job in a produce factory, where his job was to chop fruits and vegetables eight hours a day. Everything was fancy about this cafeteria, even the salad, so I ate it all the time. I invited my mom one day to lunch and I showed her my place of work. She was not only in awe of my new workspace but in awe that I was actually working there, and no one stopped me at the door. I really didn't understand how big this combo was back then.

My father passed not so long after. I later heard that my father would have liked coming with my mom that day to see where I worked. I should have invited him too, but now he was gone; I could no longer take him to see what I did. I could no longer take him to see where his hard work ended up. He would never be able to taste how the simple lettuce he chopped turned into the most delicious Caesar salad. If he could just see all these people in heels, eating it all up. If he could just see me. It was too late. If you are able, bring your parent to work one day. Introduce them to your colleagues. Colleagues, say "Hi," too! Your parents might not understand what you do, but I guarantee they understand that whatever you are doing is indirectly a result of their work too.

You shouldn't need a special day to do this either. As I found out, that day may never come. Hug and show off your loved ones while they are here on earth. If you are not able to show them off in person, keep their memories going.

This is my dad, Juan. He, along with my mom, gave me a better life. He also chopped lettuce and did it with a smile.

Love is Love

When my real father died of cancer decades ago, the life I knew with a blood father was gone. My mother was only 41, and my brothers and I were teens and not sure what to make of everything. We were fatherless and a bit angry at life. Just like that, mom took on two roles and before long and against the entire family's wishes—she remarried. It was hard to accept someone else into our lives.

Up until recently, we referred to him as "mom's husband" and he never countered that. He didn't push himself on us; he gave us space. When we'd take pictures, he'd kindly offer to take the picture. When we'd bring up the past, he'd quietly just listen, never saying a word. He didn't make mom take down the pictures of dad. He'd buy us our favorite goodies time and time and again and if we needed gardening, he'd show up before sunrise and there he was making our homes beautiful, leaving goodies at our door over and over. He asked us for nothing in return.

For years, he has been there, by mom's side, taking care of our most precious gift—mom. Here he is planting her favorite rare Pitaya cactus. He spoils her like that. I think dad would have liked him. Mom was right in listening to her heart on this one. Love is love.

Tio Pedro

Not only was I the first in my family to have an office job but I was the first in my family to travel. I was barely 18 when I was asked by my manager if I could go to Los Angeles from the Bay Area to manage a tradeshow booth. I grew up with old school, immigrant parents who didn't even let me spend the night at a cousin's house. I wondered how in the world I was going to travel 300 miles alone? My parents did not know this was standard in the "office world"; luckily for me, my mother worked in the warehouse of my place of work and the owner of the company made my mother feel at ease ... who then made my father feel at ease. I was relieved because I was afraid at 18 to ask my parents for "permission". Quite honestly, I would have said no, had it not been for that discussion between an owner that knew I could represent the company well and a humble mom that just needed to hear it from someone she trusted and respected. My mom could not say no. Phew. So, I went.

For the first time, I flew alone (free peanuts—what a luxury)! No fancy cab or uber to pick me up though; my uncle Pedro picked me up in his old landscaping pick-up truck. I also didn't end up staying at a fancy hotel even though the company would have paid for it; but I did stay on my Uncle Pedro's old couch in east Los Angeles. A little different, but believe me when I say that I felt like I was living large.

For a couple days, I set up the booth; I spoke to potential buyers, and gave it my all with a smile from ear to ear. I got back to the bay area energized because I had discovered a whole new world (that even paid for my lunch). I had a new perspective and from then on, I did not stop traveling and my parents never stopped me from going anywhere after this. How could they? It was different but it was good. Friends, get to know the cultures of those around you. Provide insights that will help others expand their knowledge of you. I know it's uncomfortable but go against the grain, if need be, especially if you know in your heart it's for the better. Parents need to see that there is value in us leaving the house, for school, life, or work. Not doing so, may limit us. Remember, they want a better life for us! Not only can it be better for you but it's better for the family! For those new to this world, there are family conversations that need to be had. Breathe deep. For those bringing in diverse talent, give us a day or so, because we have a family conversation to coordinate.

I never stayed in East Los Angeles again, although I will always remember my first business trip. No fancy hotel, just an old pick-up truck, a humble uncle willing to be my taxi, a couch, and parents that opened their eyes to something different because an amazing human made them see that their daughter was capable.

The Non-Believers

What else do you know how to do? I was asked this at 19 years old by a manager, as a last resort, who was trying to keep me working for him. He wanted me to be afraid of leaving. I left anyway. Yes, I made mistakes, but I learned. With every experience I became more confident. I developed a deep understanding of what I liked and didn't, of what I wanted to do more of and not at all. You only know what you've experienced. The only way to know if you like something or not is if you try it. Have the confidence to try something you've never done before and get your answer.

At 19, my answer to the manager that tried to hold me back was truthful. "I don't know what else I can do, but I am going to be ok." Be ok with not knowing, but if you have that gut YES feeling, be ok with the absolute worst-case scenario and do it anyways. What you know and what you end up liking might surprise you ... and everyone else.

If I can Buy a Truck

I was 19 and wore any hat given to me. I was a Purchasing Agent, Office Manager, Donut-Getter, Whatever-Was-Needed Person, at an office cubicle company in the Silicon Valley. I had no experience in this industry. Heck, no one really did. Tech was new and the area was growing. My job was to make sure production had all the pieces to build working cubicles for the new techies in the area.

The team was small, you did what was needed to meet the committed delivery deadlines, and one of those needs was coordinating the delivery of cubicles to the many tech companies popping up in the valley. As a result, we couldn't keep up. The trucks we subcontracted were not available fast enough. It was time. We had to buy our own truck. Well, to make cubicles, you needed to know how much wood to buy for the desks, how much paint it took to make the cabinets shiny, and an accurate count of screws to hold them all together. I learned that. It only made sense that I was put on point to "drive" the purchase of the company semi-truck, right? Purchasing is purchasing but I was so stressed inside. Still, I said yes.

I knew nothing about buying vehicles. Truth is, I had an old, rusty $600 Chevy truck with bald out tires in the parking lot. I built my biceps while I turned the steering wheel. I knew nothing about semi-trucks, but someone had to do it.

And just like that, the project was mine. At 19, I purchased a $100K+, 18-wheeler for our company. I was asked questions I knew nothing about, but I figured it out (no Google back then, by the way) and before long a shiny, 18-wheeler with new tires was pulling up in the docks of our warehouse. I did that! I learned that.

That year, my old rusty chevy truck was passed on to a relative and I purchased my first new car too. No one in my family had ever had a new car. We don't have to know the job exactly. We just have to want to do it and learn what it takes. If you are interested, say yes, even if you've never done it, and you will figure it out and learn from it. Also, just because no one has done it, does not mean YOU can't be the first.

P.S. I ended up at one of those nice tech companies a few years later...ha!

Entering Tech

You would think my entry into the world of technology was well thought out. A specific plan to one day enter this environment. No. Not at all. For me, the experience I had gained as a young person helped set me up for this path. I had fundamentals that were needed to start...the rest was up to me. I worked hard and allowed others to guide me.

Sand Or Sound/ Potato Or Potatoe

I was 23 and had just left a very toxic environment in the office furniture industry and I needed money. Back then there was no Google, no LinkedIn, we relied on friends and agencies to help us find jobs. I had a phone interview with one of those agencies and my phone reception was bad (landlines with phone cords, ugh), but I proceeded with the choppy phone call. They said that there was a job doing this, that, and the other at a "SAND" blaster company. Despite the reception, the talk felt great.

We both agreed this could work; me, thinking in my head, I'm going into the materials business. A few days later I started the job. I had heard "SAND" on my bad phone line, but when I arrived it turned out to be a "SOUND" company that was in the tech industry. I didn't run. I was going to adapt like I had done with everything else in my life up to that point; it was a job after all. Plus, the environment from the get-go felt good. I followed my gut and went with the flow. That was my start into the Silicon Valley tech industry.

My resume was not 100% perfect, and I didn't know everything. As a matter of fact, I hadn't even finished college because I couldn't afford to. I knew zero about tech. What I did know was, this was not a job as a doctor or a lawyer; not all my checkmarks were necessary. The things they wanted me to do, I could do. And the recruiter had a good gut feeling, and I did too. I asked a lot of questions and was very curious and adapted as the business adapted. "Adapted" being the keyword. Tech changes all the time, if there's ever an industry that is constantly changing, it's this one. You don't check all the boxes—no problem. What does matter is asking yourself; does it feel good? Can you adapt? YOUR GUT IS GOLDEN—listen to it. Sometimes the only check mark you need is a mutual "feels good". I have been in this industry for decades. I have seen computers go from the size of refrigerators to fitting in your hand. I've seen boxes with technology that once filled store aisles transform into clouds. If my landline came in clear the day I spoke to the recruiter, I might have said no. I would have gotten into my own head about what I didn't have versus not being afraid and focusing on what I did have.

Lesson learned! Was this fate? Maybe. With this job, I broke my family's poverty cycle and I hope others learn from my experience and change their lives and the lives of the generations that come after them. Sand, Sound /Potato, Potatoe- it's all the same difference.

Signs

Life goes fast and we do too. We may go our whole lives ignoring what we feel inside and the signs around us. We take for granted the nudges in our heart, the tightness in our tummy, and even the in-our-face messages that are put right in front of us, time and time again. We're moving so fast; we never stop to listen – we never stop to see until one day, we have no other choice but to notice.

The Loquat and The Ladder

We lost my uncle Julian a few years ago. He was the glue to our family. As a matter of fact, when my father died, he was the first person I called—that's how important he was. As kids we lived only blocks away from him. With his nine kids and an open door, his home was always alive. When anyone needed anything, we just showed up, no questions were asked.

My father loved visiting, but he would never show up without a gift of some sort. Between our homes, conveniently located was a little store. For a few coins, dad filled his pockets with dozens of one cent candies which was his gift for the family's children. He did this so often that I learned to never arrive anywhere without a gift.

After the candy was handed out, we all played around the big loquat tree located right at the entrance of his home. That tree was the home base for our many made-up games. It was the home base for my family. The years passed, as they do. On the day of his burial, I was so busy, the kind of busy that you can barely breathe. I didn't even have time to buy flowers. I couldn't believe on this very important day, I was going to show up without anything to offer. The drive there was uncomfortable and all I kept thinking was I had no flowers to bring- nothing. I got caught in the cycle of life and I couldn't even set aside a few minutes to get one last gift for my uncle. I kept driving.

With one of my cousins and my brother in the car, we went on our way to the funeral, empty-handed. I mentioned to them how uneasy I felt. We kept driving.

As we got closer, I decided to look on the side of the road. I slowed down. Out of the corner of my eye would you believe I saw the biggest loquat tree—just there, smack in the middle of an empty field! I had never noticed it before.

We pulled over and got out of the car. I opened the trunk and grabbed bags. Where did those bags come from? We grabbed them and ran to the tree; it was huge! Too big for us to reach any branches. Now what? We looked around, and would you believe, laying there was a ladder? A ladder and a loquat tree--that's it! Huh? Exactly what we needed. I felt something magical had just happened. It freaked me out a little.

We climbed the ladder, filled the bags, and headed to the funeral. There were enough loquat branches to go around. At the burial, there was music, friends, and family; it had a hint of our childhood. We offered the loquat branches to anyone who might need one; we ate the fruit and with his body present, we told stories of times that were now just beautiful memories of the past. My uncle was at peace. I think dad had a little something to do with this gift orchestration too. Well played Apa.

That day, I learned that the universe gives us gifts. Gifts of moments, gifts of opening of doors, gifts of good people, loquats, ladders, lessons, time, and even candy— all magic. Often, we move too fast to notice these magical wonders. Slow down. Look around. Notice the gifts. Maybe they've always been there but we just never noticed.

Look Up

SIGNS are all around us, we just have to slow down and pay attention to see them! This is that time and this is my story. When my father was alive, he used to eat the seeds from the inside of the vines from this tree. In Spanish it's called "gauje." It's a wild tree and I had typically seen it on roadsides and in rural places. I buried this detail of my father the day he was buried. I have visited my father's grave for almost 30 years, and I had never noticed that next to his grave was the biggest "guaje" tree I had ever seen. It was 30 times the size of any I can recall. How could I have missed this? I have been visiting his grave for 30 years! Had I never looked up, had it been there all along? It had to be. I kneeled next to my father's grave that day and I looked up at the tree and couldn't stop staring. I was perplexed, but there it was: Green, bright, and right next to me. I cried. Why hadn't I seen it? Why didn't I ever notice? It was so beautiful and so meaningful. It was real.

Signs exist, they're all around us. Sometimes we can't see them, but they've always been there. They wait for the right moment, perhaps for stillness and the right state of mind for us to have no other explanation but to accept them. I get it, I see it. I believe it.

Step In

I grew up across the street from a creek. This creek was basically every neighborhood kid's "swimming pool" and our parents' conveniently located babysitter. When the water was high, we would use it for rock skipping practice. I am a pretty good rock skipper. We would collect baby frogs, also called pollywogs, and put them in jars for our parents. But when the water was low, we would venture into the creek to find pockets of water holes that we could use as a personal pool to cool off on hot summer days.

On one of those hot summer days, my brother Carlos and I ran down to the creek and found one of these holes. He was about five and I was seven. The hole couldn't have been wider than four feet. He jumped in and within seconds was gasping for air and desperately waving his hands back and forth. Between swallows of dirty creek water, he managed to call out my name, "Martha! Martha!" He was getting sucked in. I was losing my brother quickly. What do I do, what do I do? I panicked and I don't know how I did it, but I pulled him out. I have been afraid of water ever since that day.

Throughout my life, I've had the great fortune to have traveled to amazing beaches, been to places with amazing pools. I am so grateful but at these amazing places I would always stay out of the water. I'd joke to cover my fear and use the excuse, "I am a land lizard," and sit in my chair listening to laughter that I am never a part of. I would ask myself: How many more times was I going to miss out? How many opportunities would I have with these amazing humans to laugh and be a part of?

Not so long ago, I took a few days off to pause a bit. We were staying at a place with a nice pool. My girls and I walked to the pool and to their surprise instead of sitting out and doing things "land lizards" do, I stood on the pool steps. I PAUSED. My daughters were a bit confused as to why I was standing there in the water. I don't know why I said this, but I said, "What do I do?" I guess I just needed reassurance that "they had me." What I heard next was exactly what I needed to hear. I hear these very simple words STEP IN, WE GOT YOU - that's it, just step in. Yes, they had me.

One of my daughters held my hand and the other stood in front of me and just like that, I took my first step into something I had been avoiding most of my life. They laughed nervously at first, I did too, but within minutes I was enjoying this moment. I had the most amazing time with my girls during this random non-particular day of pausing. We laughed like no other time, and yes, we did it in the water. We never know why people do and don't do things. Life is short, tomorrow is not promised. Fear may keep you from amazing opportunities; step in. Just one step at a time. Stepping in is easier when others have you. Pausing is a good thing. Laugh, laugh, laugh any moment you can.

Reflecting Back

BEHIND THE SMILE- a general reflection

I smile. I smile a lot. Why? Well, I am grateful of course but the truth is, it's great to have teeth. Every time someone has complimented my smile, I silently think to myself, "if they only knew." Well, what IF they knew ...

The village I was born in had no running water, the only water source was a river and was also everyone's "bathtub." It was also where people washed dirty cloth diapers, where our drinking water came from, where animals walked through. No wonder some of the villagers' smiles were hidden. Their heads bent down if they laughed or their palm over their mouth. Smiling was a reminder of the conditions of the reality they lived. I lived there too. We lived and survived on contaminated water. Lack of teeth color, and missing teeth equated to a lack of confidence. Was this my future, since it is how I started my life?

When we came to the states, the only home we could afford was $90 a month. It had no sink in the bathroom making it challenging to keep up with the daily teeth tasks and with no insurance; teeth were last on the list. BUT we finally had good water!!!! A nice green hose outside too. Moving on up.

Then my parents got jobs but no dental insurance at any of them. It had to be me. With my first work insurance, I started the process of getting my teeth in order. I was grateful for that insurance (something many underserved kids do not have the privilege of having). My smile got bigger and bigger. If you see adults, children with gold or silver on their teeth, no teeth, not smiling, or their palms covering their laughter, just know there might be a story. There always is. Be kind.

If you see someone smiling from ear to ear, this is gratitude, and it's proof that someone is feeling so so so blessed to have been given the opportunity to SMILE, so SMILE back. As you offer benefits to attract diverse talent, know that it's beyond the free snacks and coffee. You're not selling dental, you're selling smiles! You're selling confidence. You're changing lives. Where you start does not dictate where you end up. I am proof.

This Is Not Bakersfield

As a kid, the only vacations I can remember were hopping in our non-air-conditioned station wagon (no seatbelt) and making the trek down to the Central Valley for the weekend. These "vacations" typically were in triple digit heat since that's when the fruits and veggies were ready for picking. My extended family primarily worked in agriculture: Cherries, oranges, carrots.

I vividly remember a young girl about four, sitting on the dirt ground eating carrots. They were straight from the land, and all tangled together in what appeared to be some sort of bouquet. Her face was smudged with dirt from the dust that surrounded her. Her bare feet were dirty from the ground she stepped on. All the families' houses were hot too; no air conditioning, but we ran and got dirty and played to the point of exhaustion. Our faces were smudged with dirt and tummies full of carrots.

These were my vacations. Dirt, heat, no air conditioning, family, fruit, veggies—I knew no different. Now that I'm older, I sit here in amazement of how far we can go. How far people can take us by exposing us to different places and I hope that little girl who sat on the dirt ground, her face smudged with dirt, eating carrots is sitting somewhere having a cup of coffee and appreciating life and how far she's come. I am.

Speaking & Believing

It's hard to talk about our shame but sometimes it's necessary. I never knew that one day speaking raw about my story would be the healing key that would unlock, not only the belief in me, but belief in something bigger.

Lessons from Charlie Chaplin

SPEAKING – "When he was silent—everyone laughed, when he spoke everyone was silent." I grew up in a little town named Niles. Niles was the original Hollywood back in the early 1900s. Black and white silent films were all the rage. Charlie Chaplin was its most famous star. However, with new technology, sound came into the picture. What would it sound like if Charlie spoke? In 1940 Charlie got his chance to show us. The world was intrigued.

In his first sound movie, "The Great Dictator" he played a barber who looks like the not-so-liked leader. That not-so-liked leader is supposed to give a speech. We can all imagine what that speech would be. With the confusion, he receives pressure from the fellow next to him. This humble barber (Charlie) is pushed to get up and talk. A man next to him said, "You must speak." He said, "I can't." The man said, "You must, it's our only hope." Charlie said one word, "HOPE," and he walked up to the microphone and began. He used this once in a lifetime moment (maybe for the film, maybe for the world) to speak words about peace, kindness, and humanity. In this moment

Charlie proved he was not only a silent, funny guy, but that he was a human with a platform and an opportunity. With words, he could give hope.

His speech, which is over 80 years old, is still relevant today. Kindness is still relevant today. Peace is still relevant today. Humanity is still relevant today. I never knew the power of voice until recently, because I was silent for most of my life. It's not the quantity of times you speak but the quality of the words that are used.

Use your power; your opportunity; your voice for good. That's it. Good is always quality.

Believing

I never thought my life stories could help others. For decades, I considered my stories shameful because who talks about getting smuggled across the border around the water cooler? That said, I was blessed to be in workplaces with a water cooler. I was proud of those places, and I wanted to show them off. Whenever I got a chance, I would sign up to give tours during my lunch time.

One day, on one of those tours, a group of kids from the surrounding agriculture farms came to our company, and I was their guide. I was doing what I did, showing them the beautiful buildings, the nice conference rooms, and even the basketball court that was between the buildings. One of the kids looked around and, with tears in his eyes, said to me, "This is great but kids like me are not at places like this." Little did he know I wasn't just a guide, I was him and I was there. I needed to tell him.

That was the first time I spoke about my REAL story and where I came from, and I sugar-coated nothing. Although I had been working at these amazing places for decades, it was that moment right there that I put my shame aside and turned it into hope. Others could be there, and I was proof.

A few months later, another opportunity came my way. By this time, I had been at Adobe (the Photoshop company) for over 15 years. The company sent out a message asking for diversity stories for an opportunity to speak on stage in front of 1200 Adobe leaders. A few would be selected; Adobe has 25,000 employees— what are the chances? All they needed was a short submission. A short submission seemed easy enough, but this was not a business talk. This submission would be an admission! They were looking for a life story. LIFE? I immediately thought to myself, if they only knew my life. The negative thoughts about my background silenced me and I did not submit anything. Days passed and I couldn't stop thinking about it. I always wanted to speak, for decades, I've watched countless motivators, performers, executives do their thing from a stage. I always sat in the audience wondering "what if?" Then I would start the negative talk: You're not pretty enough, skinny enough, smart enough, educated enough. You're from a shack, you're smuggled, you're poor, you were kicked out of school. I had no business dreaming of ever speaking on a stage.

But I liked that dream. The deadline for submissions was getting closer and I confided in a couple of my friends. Like many of the good people in my life who have ever pushed me forward, they too encouraged me. I also thought about my two daughters and what advice I'd give them if there was a chance at their dream.

In that moment, I hit SUBMIT to my "admission." I waited. A few months passed. I got an email that read in the subject line, You've Been Chosen.

Oh shoot, what did I do? I could still back out. With a deep breath, I accepted what was in front of me and although it was scary and something I've been told not to talk about—I was going to speak.

What was I going to say? Everything? Was I going to sugar-coat it? The writing process began. I can't tell you how many times I cried during this process, but little by little the cries turned into strength. My story was not a story of shame like I had felt when I told the boy on that tour; my story was about hope. I just didn't know it then.

I had a couple months to practice. The story writing process was grueling; what stays, what goes. This process of making sense of one's life was incredibly healing for me. It was also incredibly stressful, I had to fit my life story into a few minutes. Minutes! I had been alive for 46 years. How can I squeeze that into minutes? I kept working at it, writing and rewriting. Once I felt semi decent with the written story, I now had to get the words out of my body that I had never spoken and nonetheless in front of some of the smartest people I knew. I sought help everywhere to sharpen my speaking skills ... I had to. I knew nothing. What do we do when we know nothing? Yep,

YOUTUBE! I also read books. I sought feedback from people I knew well and from people who barely knew me. I needed the story to make sense to as many people as possible. One of the best pieces of advice was from a complete stranger. He said, "Just speak from the heart." HEART—that was a concept I could get behind. During this time, I was also given the gift of an amazing speaking coach from my company. His name is Jason. He had experience and spoke to thousands all the time. He looked zero like me, but it didn't matter. He was patient and guided me in a way that I understood. He said, breathe, drink water, speak Spanish. He gave me a final blessing with three words; he believed my story was as good as it could be. He said, "YOU ARE READY." I believed I was ready too. Jason was not only a coach, but he was also a believer. We all need believers. That day changed my life. I spoke my truth in front of 1200 amazing technology professionals. The CEO was front and center—no pressure! My family sat next to him. My mother sat there too, with tears in her eyes she watched the little girl she once hid, stand there in the brightest pink shirt you can imagine doing exactly what she feared her whole life—SPEAK. Mom's risk of leaving "The Other Side" had paid off. That day, every word I spoke fell off my body, like shame dripping from my heart. I was not hiding, I couldn't. I wasn't silent. I was me and now everyone knew it. That day too, the CEO came to congratulate me. He also hugged my mother. She had no idea who he was, but like many Latinos do, she hugged him right back. I don't have a picture of that but it's an image in my head that I will never forget. This was a humanity image.

It's been a few years and I haven't stopped speaking or writing. Both things I had never done before. At 46, I had found a passion for hope with words. I was learning new things and I liked it! I would not be able to write my stories so openly if I did not feel safe. Feeling safe is so important. I also would not be able to believe in myself without the relentless belief in me from others. My believers have always pushed me forward.

Although there has been a combination of negative and positive people in my life. I was attracted to positive people like a magnet. Who isn't? It feels good. I tried to pay more attention to positive words versus negative ones; this ratio is important. Be good frequently and tell others positive words often. This is especially important in communities where love with words is not part of our everyday lives. Although many have seen value in me, it wasn't until I believed that I was valuable myself that everything clicked. I remember a few days after I spoke my story, a young man by the name of Martin wanted to meet me. I agreed. When I saw him, his eyes watered and when he hugged me, he was shaking. We proceeded to have coffee and he told me how impactful seeing me on a big Silicon Valley stage was for him. I had no idea that this would be the beginning of many conversations, many talks I'd have with people like Martin. It was addictive to have people believe they too could be bigger, better, and they could do it all by being themselves. This was hope. My story stopped being about me and had now turned into a story for others.

I couldn't give up on others. I kept speaking, talking, and writing. Good was all over the place and I could feel it. I was confident in what I was saying because it had happened to me. It was the truth. I was living proof that it was possible; that where we came from was only that—where we came from. That with good people, we can dream big and big is a possibility. That despite all odds, we could be there too.

Martin proceeded to show me a passage in a book over coffee that day. Ironically this passage was called YOUR STORY. Seriously, this was wild. He read it to me. He believed our meeting was no coincidence. He said it was God. God talks in the office? Yes. I've had my issues with believing in God, so him telling me this perplexed me. With so many obstacles in my life, quite frankly you sometimes have your doubts. When I mentioned this doubt, he didn't judge me. He said to me, "Ok, just know, God is Good." Good was a concept I could get behind. I kept following good. Good was addictive and just like that I started seeing serendipitous interconnections with everyone I had ever met, with everything I had ever done, and with everything that had happened.

Good was real. Thank you, Martin. I am a believer.

Whatever you believe in. God, Gods, Creator, Angels, Spirit, Guides, Mystical One, Holy Spirit, Universe, Rocks, Aliens - it's all GOOD. Just be real, be kind, and be accepting of each other. There are millions of stories we have never heard that are from the "The Other Side." They are important because they are the TRUTH. If we don't know the truth, how can we ever fix anything?

My name is Martha—I am a Mexican immigrant. My parents wanted a better life for me, and it wasn't easy but with good people I have it. Peace, Love, Humanity and Opportunity everyone.

Silicon Valley

[silicon valley] NOUN

the area in northern California, southwest
of San Francisco in the Santa Clara valley
region, where many of the high-technology
companies are concentrated.

The Other Side

I've been on the other side, where loved ones cried their
last goodbyes
I've been on the other side, where I've fallen despite the
tries
I've been on the other side, where kind words were just
not heard
I've been on the other side, where I was told to not say a
word.

I've been on the other side, where better was just a dream
I've been on the other side, where that job didn't quite
seem
I've been on the other side, by myself and all alone
I've been on the other side, where my home was not my
own.

I've come out the other side, greeted with hope and openly
hugged
I've come out the other side, guided with smiles and
unconditionally loved
I've come out the other side, ready to show what I've got
I've come out the other side, but not for once have I forgot.

Martha Niño Rodriguez

About the
Author

Martha Niño Rodriguez is a Mexican born, 20+ year Latina Silicon Valley Industry Professional. She is part of the few Latinos in this industry. In her words, "We need more." She has always been fascinated by speakers, motivators, and the stage. She never thought one day she would get the opportunity to be on one herself. Her chance came and it was fate. With the help of many believers, she spoke her story for the first time and since then she has not stopped speaking, motivating, and writing. Her story was not a conventional Silicon Valley story, it was a story of a child that was smuggled into the United States passing as a stranger's daughter, how she lived in poverty, how she was kicked out of school, how her father died, and how despite all the obstacles in her life, with good people she now has a better life. Her path to the Silicon Valley was not a straight line; it couldn't be. With no money and a lack of educational guidance, the odds of success were low. She beat the odds. With her stories and reflections of her life experiences she hopes that others believe they can beat theirs too. She also hopes others can see value in underserved children and communities and consider the unspoken story of the silent; a story that is coming from "The Other Side."

Made in USA - Kendallville, IN
66943_9798362830410
08.10.2023 1408